The Sea

Behold the wonders of the mighty deep,
Where crabs and lobsters learn to creep,
And little fishes learn to swim,
And clumsy sailors tumble in.

Anonymous

Little People™ Big Book

About
THE SEA

ALEXANDRIA, VIRGINIA

Table of Contents

By the Sea

Shore
> *Poem by Mary Britton Miller* 5

Did You Ever Wonder About the Sea
> *Fascinating Facts* 6

A Fish Wish
> *Story by Michael J. Pellowski* 8

A Walk on the Beach
> *Fascinating Facts* 12

The Walrus and the Carpenter
> *Poem by Lewis Carroll* 14

Life in the Sea

Fish
> *Poem by Mary Ann Hoberman* 19

If You Ever
> *Traditional Poem* 20

Hide and Seek Under the Sea
> *Hidden Picture Game* 21

The Fish With the Deep Sea Smile
> *Poem by Margaret Wise Brown* 24

Giants of the Sea
> *Fascinating Facts* 28

Baby Beluga
> *Song by Raffi and Debi Pike* 32

Sailing on the Sea

Sea Shell
Poem by Amy Lowell 35
The Owl and the Pussycat
Poem by Edward Lear 36
Did You Ever Wonder About Pirates
Fascinating Facts 40
Pirate Treasure Hunt
Hidden Picture Game 42
The Vision in the Snow
Story by Holling Clancy Holling 44
A Sailor Went to Sea
Clapping Game 46

The Magic of the Sea

Undersea
Poem by Marchette Chute 49
A Doll's Adventure at Sea
Story by Stephanie St. Pierre 50
Simply Silly Seaside Riddles
Riddle Activity 56
Merla the Mischievous Mermaid
Story by Laura Hitchcock 58

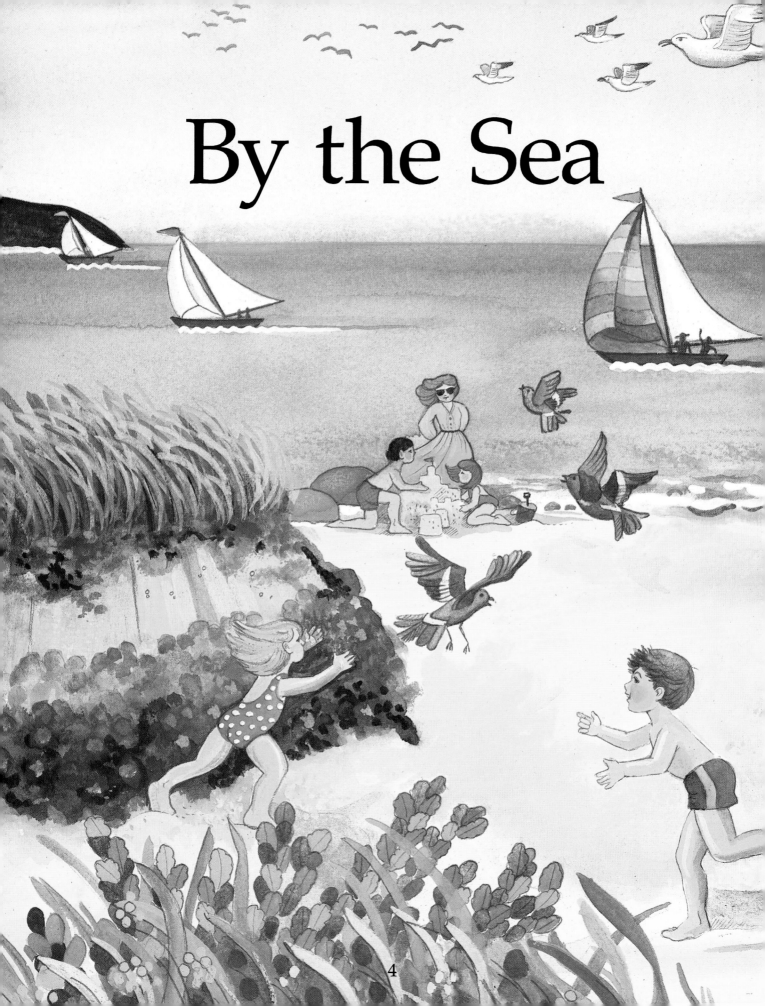

By the Sea

Shore

Play on the seashore
And gather up shells,
Kneel in the damp sands
Digging wells.

Run on the rocks
Where the seaweed slips,
Watch the waves
And the beautiful ships.

Mary Britton Miller

DID YOU EVER WONDER
ABOUT THE SEA

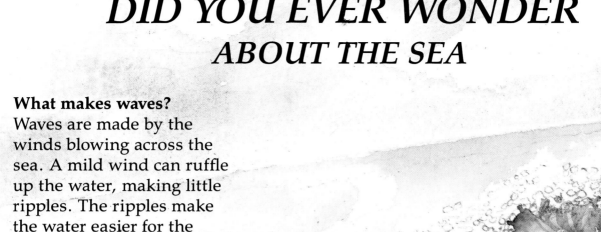

What makes waves?
Waves are made by the
winds blowing across the
sea. A mild wind can ruffle
up the water, making little
ripples. The ripples make
the water easier for the
wind to catch. Soon the
wind blows the ripples into
little wavelets. Sometimes a
wavelet merges with other
wavelets, which makes a
bigger wave. The farther
the wave goes, the bigger it
gets, because it picks up
other waves along the way.

What is seaweed?
Seaweed is the grass of the
ocean. It provides food for
sea creatures and adds
oxygen to the water so fish
and other animals can
breathe. Seaweed can be
green, blue-green, brown,
or red. Look for it washed
up on the beach, or floating along the top of the
water. In some parts of the
world, people eat seaweed.
It is sometimes used to
make toothpaste.

What is sand?

A grain of sand is made from rocks that are broken into tiny pieces and worn down by the wind and the tides of the ocean. Pick up a handful of sand and look closely at the tiny grains. It takes billions of these miniature rocks to make a beach of sand. If you look on the beach, you may also find small stones and pebbles that have been worn smooth by the ocean —they're on their way to becoming sand, too!

What are seashells?

A seashell is the hard outer skeleton of a mollusk. Mollusks are sea creatures like clams, oysters, and mussels. Some mollusks have one shell, shaped like a spiral. Others have two shells that shut like a box to protect the mollusk's soft body. The shells you look for and collect on the beach were once part of mollusks. Now all that's left of them are the shells.

The best time to look for shells is when the tide is going out or right after a storm.

A Fish Wish
by Michael J. Pellowski

ittle Joey Jenkins sat on his blue beach blanket and watched waves roll up the shore toward him. Except for Joey and his mom the whole beach was deserted. Joey looked around and sighed.

"What's wrong, Joey?" his mom asked.

"I have nothing to do," Joey replied. "I wish I could meet some friends."

"Today is a rare day indeed," his mom said. "We are the only ones on the beach. Maybe it is a magic day."

Joey got up and started to walk down the beach. "I wish some friends would appear," he chuckled.

"Maybe you can make friends with some fish," his mom teased.

"I wish I could," Joey laughed as he strolled along. A bit later Joey spied something strange lying on the sand. It was a large, funny-looking seashell. Joey picked it up. "I wonder if I can hear the sea," said Joey as he put the shell to his ear. But what Joey heard wasn't the sea.

"Put me down!" a voice in the shell yelled.

Joey gasped, dropped the shell, and jumped back in alarm. "D-Did you speak?" sputtered Joey.

"Of course I spoke," the voice boomed back. "But I said put me down, not drop me on my face! Come here and turn me over!"

Joey gulped. Cautiously, he crept over to the shell and turned it open side up. Then, as Joey watched in surprise, a crab poked its head out of the hole in the shell.

8

"PA-TOOEY!" grumbled the crabby crab. "Thanks to you I got sand in my mouth!"

"Sorry," said Joey. "B-But how can you talk? Are you magic?"

"Well, I can't pull a halibut out of a hat, but I'm magic sure enough," replied the crab.

"Magic!" muttered Joey. "Then you could grant me a wish."

"I sure could," said the crab. "In fact, I could grant you two wishes. And I will! Wish away, sonny."

Joey gave a wish some thought. He remembered the wish he'd made minutes ago about making friends with the fish. A smile spread across his face. "I wish I were a fish," he cried.

"Close your eyes," ordered the crab. Joey giggled and obeyed. "Fiddle dee dee," sang the magic crab. "If it's a fish you want, a fish you'll be!"

POOF! SPLASH! GLUB! When Joey opened his eyes he was bobbing beneath the waves.

"I'm a fish," Joey chuckled as he swam around and around. "Look at me! I'm a fish!"

"Clam up and calm down," instructed a big flounder. "You're making too much commotion. You'll attract the bigger fish and they'll have you for lunch!"

"I'd like to have lunch with a big fish," replied Joey.

"You'll be the lunch," said the leader of a school of angelfish. Suddenly, the entire school of angelfish darted away.

"Why did they leave in such a hurry?" Joey said. When he looked behind him he knew the answer. A big, hungry fish was headed right at him.

"Yeow!" Joey cried as he shut his eyes. "I wish I weren't a fish anymore!"

POOF! "Wake up, Joey," said his mom as she tapped on Joey's arm. "It's time to leave."

Joey opened his eyes. He was lying on his towel on the shore.

"It was only a dream," chuckled Joey as he got up and prepared to leave. "It was all a dream."

"Aren't you taking that home?" asked Joey's mom as she pointed at the funny-looking seashell near her son. Joey looked at the shell. It was the magic one in his dream.

"N-No," sputtered Joey. "That shell belongs here."

Joey and his mom started up the beach. As they walked away, Joey glanced back at the shell. Was it a dream? he wondered. Joey wasn't sure. He was even less sure when he thought he heard a voice from the shell call, "Good-bye!"

A WALK ON THE BEACH

What can you find at the sea by the shore?
Seaweed and hermit crabs, driftwood and more!
You can find seashells wherever you wish,
Footprints of sea gulls and bright jellyfish,
Pebbles as smooth as a jewel in your hand,
All shaped by the wind and the sea and the sand.

Let's take a walk on the beach and see what else we can find.

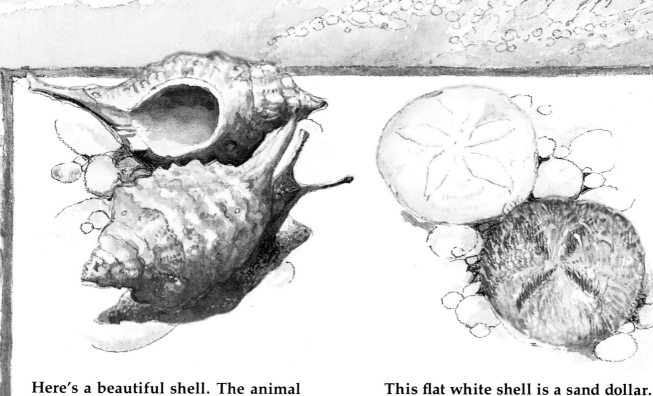

Here's a beautiful shell. The animal that lives inside it is called a whelk. The long, skinny part of the shell holds a siphon, or straw. When the whelk moves through mud and sand, it pushes its siphon out into clear water to drink.

This flat white shell is a sand dollar. A living sand dollar is an animal that lives in the ocean. The sand dollar's shell is covered with tiny, short spines, and it has many short little feet shaped like tubes.

The scary-looking shell above used to have a horseshoe crab inside it! When a young horseshoe crab starts to get big, it outgrows its shell. So it sheds it and grows a new shell (left). The cast-off shell washed up on the beach for us to find!

What is the crinkly black shell below? It's an egg case. It held the egg of a skate. Skates are sea creatures similar to sting rays. When the egg hatches, the baby skate swims out of the case with its fins folded over its body.

This funny round shell doesn't look like a skeleton, but that's what it is! It's the skeleton of a sea urchin. A sea urchin is a spiny animal that lives in the water. The spines come in many colors though usually they are green or black.

The Walrus and the Carpenter

The sun was shining on the sea,
   Shining with all his might:
He did his very best to make
   The billows smooth and bright—
And this was odd, because it was
   The middle of the night.

The moon was shining sulkily,
   Because she thought the sun
Had got no business to be there
   After the day was done—
"It's very rude of him," she said,
   "To come and spoil the fun!"

The sea was wet as wet could be,
   The sands were dry as dry.
You could not see a cloud, because
   No cloud was in the sky:
No birds were flying overhead—
   There were no birds to fly.

The Walrus and the Carpenter
   Were walking close at hand:
They wept like anything to see
   Such quantities of sand:
"If this were only cleared away,"
   They said, "it would be grand!"

"If seven maids with seven mops
   Swept it for half a year,
Do you suppose," the Walrus said,
   "That they could get it clear?"
"I doubt it," said the Carpenter,
   And shed a bitter tear.

"O Oysters, come and walk with us!"
   The Walrus did beseech.
"A pleasant walk, a pleasant talk,
   Along the briny beach:
We cannot do with more than four,
   To give a hand to each."

14

The eldest Oyster looked at him,
    But never a word he said:
The eldest Oyster winked his eye,
    And shook his heavy head—
Meaning to say he did not choose
    To leave the oyster-bed.

But four young Oysters hurried up,
    All eager for the treat:
Their coats were brushed, their faces washed,
    Their shoes were clean and neat—
And this was odd, because, you know,
    They hadn't any feet.

Four other Oysters followed them,
    And yet another four:
And thick and fast they came at last,
    And more, and more, and more—
All hopping through the frothy waves,
    And scrambling to the shore.

The Walrus and the Carpenter
    Walked on a mile or so,
And then they rested on a rock
    Conveniently low:
And all the little Oysters stood
    And waited in a row.

"The time has come," the Walrus said,
  "To talk of many things:
Of shoes—and ships—and sealing wax—
  Of cabbages—and kings—
And why the sea is boiling hot—
  And whether pigs have wings."

"But wait a bit," the Oysters cried,
  "Before we have our chat;
For some of us are out of breath,
  And all of us are fat!"
"No hurry!" said the Carpenter.
  They thanked him much for that.

"A loaf of bread," the Walrus said,
  "Is what we chiefly need:
Pepper and vinegar besides
  Are very good indeed—
Now, if you're ready, Oysters dear,
  We can begin to feed."

"But not on us!" the Oysters cried,
  Turning a little blue.
"After such kindness, that would be
  A dismal thing to do!"
"The night is fine," the Walrus said.
  "Do you admire the view?

"It was so kind of you to come!
    And you are very nice!"
The Carpenter said nothing but
    "Cut us another slice.
I wish you were not quite so deaf—
    I've had to ask you twice!"

"It seems a shame," the Walrus said,
    "To play them such a trick.
After we've brought them out so far,
    And made them trot so quick!"
The Carpenter said nothing but
    "The butter's spread too thick!"

"I weep for you," the Walrus said:
    "I deeply sympathize."
With sobs and tears he sorted out
    Those of the largest size,
Holding his pocket-handkerchief
    Before his streaming eyes.

"O Oysters," said the Carpenter,
    "You've had a pleasant run!
Shall we be trotting home again?"
    But answer came there none—
And this was scarcely odd, because
    They'd eaten every one.

Lewis Carroll

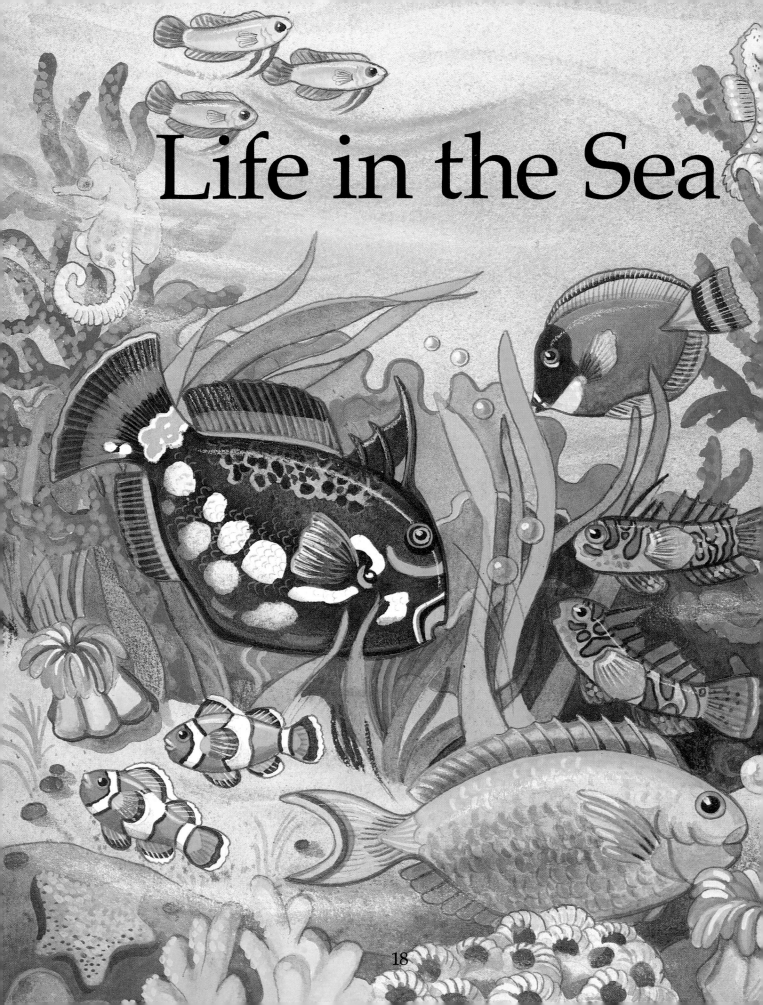

Life in the Sea

Fish

Look at them flit
Lickety-split
Wiggling
Swiggling
Curving
Hurrying
Scurrying
Chasing
Racing
Whizzing
Whisking
Flying
Frisking
Tearing around
With a leap and a bound
But none of them making the tiniest
        tiniest
      tiniest
    tiniest
  sound.

Mary Ann Hoberman

19

If You Ever

If you ever ever ever ever ever
    If you ever ever ever meet a whale,
You must never never never never never
    You must never never never touch its tail:
For if you ever ever ever ever ever
    If you ever ever ever touch its tail,
You will never never never never never
    You will never never meet another whale.

Traditional

HIDE AND SEEK UNDER THE SEA

Is that a leaf floating in the water? Or is it a fish? Some types of sea creatures have a special ability to look like something else, or to blend in with their background. This helps them to trap food and hide from their enemies. Using the clues below, can you find the sea creatures hiding on the next two pages? Look for 2 sting rays, 2 octopuses, 1 hermit crab, 3 lizard fish, 1 sailfin leaf fish, and 1 sargassum fish.

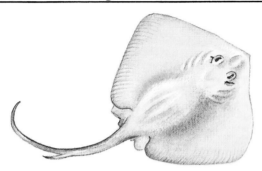

The *sting ray* is flat like a pancake. Its skin is sand-colored, so it hides on the sandy bottom of the sea.

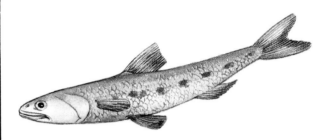

The long thin *lizard fish* is speckled just like the bottom of the ocean. That's why it likes to hide there.

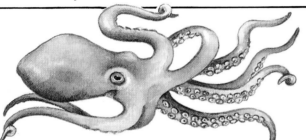

The *octopus* can change colors. When it swims through green seaweed, the octopus is green. When it swims through the depths of the ocean, it's brown!

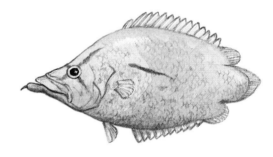

The *sailfin leaf fish* looks like a leaf floating along with the current.

The *hermit crab* lives in an empty shell. For more protection, the crab attaches an anemone to its shell. The anemone is an animal that looks like a flower.

Seaweed makes a perfect hiding place for the *sargassum fish*. Other creatures can't see the sargassum fish among the seaweed.

21

The Fish With the Deep Sea Smile

They fished and they fished
Way down in the sea,
Down in the sea a mile.
They fished among all the fish in the sea
For the fish with the deep sea smile.

One fish came up from the deep of the sea,
From down in the sea a mile.
It had blue-green eyes
And whiskers three,
But never a deep sea smile.

One fish came up from the deep of the sea,
From down in the sea a mile,
With electric lights
Up and down his tail,
But never a deep sea smile.

They fished and they fished
Way down in the sea,
Down in the sea a mile.
They fished among all the fish in the sea
For the fish with the deep sea smile.

One fish came up with terrible teeth,
One fish with long, strong jaws.
One fish came up
With long stalked eyes,
One fish with terrible claws.

They fished all through the ocean deep
For many and many a mile.
And they caught a fish
With a laughing eye,
But none with a deep sea smile.

And then one day they got a pull
From down in the sea a mile.
And when they pulled the fish
Into the boat
He smiled a deep sea smile.

And as he smiled, the hook got free
And then, with a deep sea smile
He flipped his tail
And swam away,
Down in the sea a mile.

Margaret Wise Brown

GIANTS OF THE SEA

The sea is full of many strange and unusual creatures. Some are very, very tiny—so tiny you cannot even see them without a microscope. There are also creatures in the sea that are incredibly huge—the giants of the sea.

The **blue whale** is the largest animal that has ever lived. It is even bigger than the biggest dinosaurs. It is a mammal, not a fish, which means it needs to breathe air to stay alive. There are not very many blue whales left in the world today because for a long time people hunted these whales for meat and oil and whalebone.

A full-grown blue whale can weigh as much as 250,000 pounds. That's a big number! That's more than 50 full-grown elephants!

Despite its enormous size, the blue whale is a gentle creature that eats tiny sea animals and plants called plankton.

Whales talk to each other by singing! Their songs can last as long as two hours. They sing alone, and they sing together. Whale songs are full of bubbles and squeaks and grunts and groans!

Every two or three years a mother whale gives birth to a baby whale. Baby blue whales weigh more than most cars when they are born! Mother whales take good care of their babies, swimming close to them and teaching them all about life in the sea.

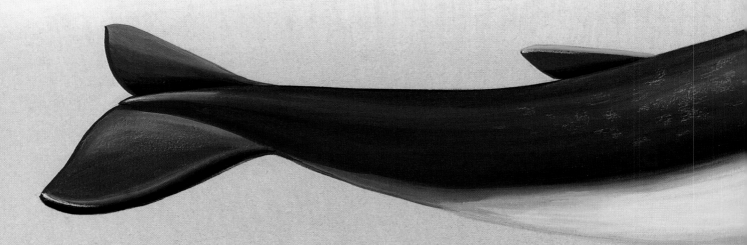

The **giant clam** lives in the South Pacific in shallow waters. Its shell is big enough for a person to sit in!

The giant clam eats mostly algae, a kind of tiny plant that lives in the water.

People like to eat giant clams, and sometimes their shells are used as birdbaths.

Rays are large, flat fish with wide "wings" and long, whiplike tails. They are close relatives of the shark.

The largest rays are manta rays, sometimes called devil rays. These enormous fish weigh thousands of pounds. From the tip of one wing to the tip of the other a ray may be 20 feet wide!

Though not quite as big as mantas, sting rays are very big fish—and they are even more dangerous! They have poisonous spines in their tails.

There are even some rays that can give off an electric shock! The electric ray carries an electric current on its wings—just like the current that goes through a wire. Fortunately the electric ray lives very far out to sea.

The **giant squid** has the largest eye of any animal, over 15 inches wide—almost as big as a car tire!

The giant squid has been known to chase and attack ships at sea. It also attacks whales. Squids use "jet power" to swim through the water. They have a special opening that lets water into their bodies. Then they use their muscles to shoot the water out again. As the water rushes out, the animal moves forward.

Surprisingly enough, the largest **sharks** of all, the whale shark and the basking shark, are not dangerous. They eat only plankton, tiny sea animals and plants.

The whale shark's egg is the largest egg of any animal. Imagine an egg the size of a car. The whale shark's egg could be that big!

The great white shark is smaller but a lot more dangerous. The jaws of some great white sharks open wide enough for a person to stand in.

Baby Beluga

Baby Beluga in the deep blue sea,
Swim so wild and swim so free,
Heaven above and the sea below,
And a little white whale on the go.

Baby Beluga, Baby Beluga,
Is the water warm,
Is your mama home,
With you so happy?

Way down yonder where the dolphins play,
Where you dive and splash all day,
Waves roll in and the waves roll out,
See the water squirtin' out of your spout.

Baby Beluga, Baby Beluga.
Sing your little song.
Sing for all your friends,
We like to hear you.

When it's dark, and you're home and fed,
Curl up snug in your water bed,
Moon is shining and the stars are out,
Good night, little whale, good night.

Baby Beluga, Baby Beluga,
With tomorrow's sun, another day's begun,
You'll soon be waking.

Baby Beluga in the deep blue sea,
Swim so wild and swim so free;
Heaven above and the sea below,
And a little white whale on the go,
You're just a little white whale on the go.

Raffi and Debi Pike

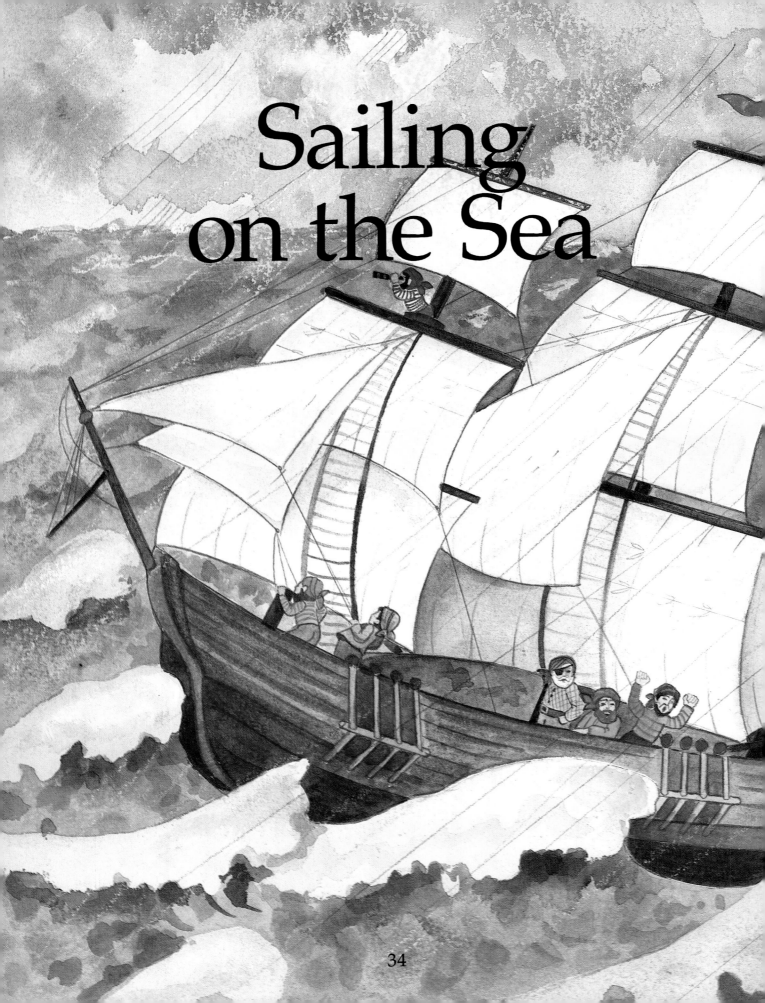

Sailing on the Sea

Sea Shell

Sea Shell, Sea Shell,
   Sing me a song, O please!
A song of ships, and sailor men,
   And parrots, and tropical trees,

Of islands lost in the Spanish Main
Which no man ever may find again,
Of fishes and corals under the waves,
And seahorses stabled in great green caves.

Sea Shell, Sea Shell,
Sing of the things you know so well.

Amy Lowell

The Owl and the Pussycat

The Owl and the Pussycat went to sea
  In a beautiful pea-green boat,
They took some honey, and plenty of money,
  Wrapped up in a five-pound note,
The Owl looked up to the stars above,
  And sang to a small guitar,
"O lovely Pussy! O Pussy, my love,
  What a beautiful Pussy you are,
                You are,
                You are,
What a beautiful Pussy you are!"

Pussy said to the Owl, "You elegant fowl!
    How charmingly sweet you sing!
O let us be married! too long have we tarried:
    But what shall we do for a ring?"
They sailed away, for a year and a day,
    To the land where the Bong-tree grows
And there in a wood a Piggy-wig stood
    With a ring at the end of his nose,
                His nose,
                His nose,
With a ring at the end of his nose.

"Dear Pig, are you willing to sell for one shilling
    Your ring?" Said the Piggy, "I will."
So they took it away, and were married next day
    By the Turkey who lives on the hill.
They dined on mince, and slices of quince,
    Which they ate with a runcible spoon;
And hand in hand, on the edge of the sand,
    They danced by the light of the moon,
            The moon,
            The moon,
They danced by the light of the moon.

Edward Lear

39

DID YOU EVER WONDER
ABOUT PIRATES

Were there really pirates?
Yes, hundreds of years ago, fierce pirates sailed the Atlantic Ocean in fast ships. They were looking for adventure—and treasure! The pirates attacked rich merchant ships and stole their gold, silver, and jewels. Often they buried their treasure along the beaches of the Atlantic coast so that no one else could find it and take it away!

Sometimes the pirates never made it back to dig up their buried treasure. Sometimes they forgot where they buried it. Other times their treasure-filled ships sank on a rocky shore during a big storm.

Who was Blackbeard?
Edward Teach was one of the scariest pirates ever to sail the seas. His nickname was Blackbeard—because of his long black beard that he liked to tie up with bright red ribbons.

Blackbeard attacked ships at sea up and down the North American coast. People said he buried lots of treasure along the beaches of North Carolina, South Carolina, and Georgia. But no one knows for sure, because it has never been found.

What was the Jolly Roger?

Many pirate ships sailed under a black flag with a white skull and crossbones on it. It was called the Jolly Roger. Sometimes the flags showed a whole skeleton or a flaming sword. Sometimes the flags were decorated with an hourglass. That meant, "Your time is up!"

The pirates hoped their flag would scare sailors on the other ships. And most of the time, it worked!

Were there any women pirates?

Yes! One was Anne Bonney, a well-educated girl from Ireland. She fell in love with a pirate named Captain John Rackham, who was known as Calico Jack. So she joined his pirate band.

Mary Read was a girl from London who went to sea. But one day her ship was captured by Calico Jack and his pirates. She became a pirate along with Anne Bonney.

PIRATE TREASURE HUNT

Ahoy there, fearless treasure hunter! Before you lies the map to Captain Big Toe's Pirate Treasure. Follow these steps with care, and you will find a chest of gold—if you're lucky.

From your lookout in the tallest tree,
Walk ten paces west.
There you'll find the Arrowhead Cave
But not the treasure chest.

Pass the giant clam shell
Not twenty paces on.
There you'll find the Cave of Skulls
But the treasure's gone.

Eight paces as the crow flies,
As sneaky as a thief,
You'll find an underwater cave.
Swim to find the coral reef.

Now swim to Bluebeard's Waterfall.
Beware—the water's dark.
Find Blue Angel Grotto
And look out for the shark!

At last you've found the treasure!
It's in Blue Angel Grotto.
Finder keepers, losers weepers,
That's a pirate's motto.

Tall Tree Lookout

Crow Pass

Bluebeard's Waterfall

Hangman's Cliff

Blue Angel Grotto

Underwater Mermaid's Cave

Shark Lagoon

Coral Reef

N
NW   NE
W   E
SW   SE
S

The Vision in the Snow
from SEABIRD by Holling Clancy Holling

The summer snowstorm not only blotted out the coast; it shut out the sun, land, and sea. Caught in a tidal current, a whaling ship ran in this white haze like a blind thing being pushed.

The keen-eyed lad, high in the crow's nest, was a worried lookout. Here he was, fourteen, a year out of New Bedford. For this whaling voyage he had signed on as the Ship's Boy. And now they trusted his searching eyes at the masthead. But how could anyone be expected to see dangerous rocks through this snow? He stamped his cold feet in the flimsy canvas barrel. Below him the mast melted into white nothing. Spars with furled sails made scarecrow arms. His lookout barrel seemed to float upward in a falling sky. . . . To Ezra Brown the world was all unreal. . . .

A shadow passed him, gone before he really saw it. It came again and was gone. Then it hovered, beyond arm's reach. A white bird soared motionless in the falling snow, looking at him. It gave no cry. It, too, was unreal to Ezra—as though the silent flakes had formed a snowy vision. The boy gazed without blinking. He had never seen anything so coldly beautiful—so much a part of snow and fog and the mystery of air. . . .

Without warning the white bird wheeled, swept forward, and shot straight up. . . . It's gone, thought Ezra. Why did it go so fast? . . . As in a dream, he remembered a playful swallow back home in Maine. It liked to fly toward a steep barn wall, then swoop upward, missing a crash by inches. And now this seabird—this ivory gull out of the Arctic—did the same thing. One minute it hung in the snow, and the next it swung out and up, like climbing a cliff—

The memory snapped Ezra out of his trance as though struck by a harpoon. Even before he felt the blast of colder air on his face, he knew. He found his voice and bellowed into the white haze—"ICEBERG! ICEBERG! DEAD AHEAD!"

A head-on collision with an iceberg has sunk many a vessel. But at Ezra's wild yells the ship swerved away in time. It scraped the ice with a shudder that nearly shook the boy from his nest. Then the Whaler went on, unharmed.

A SAILOR WENT TO SEA

This is a sea game you can play with a friend.

While you say the rhyme, clap your hands together as if you were playing "Pattycake." But whenever you say the words "see" or "sea," salute like a good sailor!

A sailor went to sea, sea, sea,
To see what he could see, see, see,
But all that he could see, see, see,
Was the bottom of the deep blue sea, sea, sea!

A sailor went to   *sea*   *sea*   *sea*

(play pattycake)   **(salute)**   **(salute)**   **(salute)**

To see what he could   see   see   see

(play pattycake again)   **(salute 3 times)**
(Repeat this game for the rest of the verse.)

The Magic of the Sea

Undersea

Beneath the waters
  Green and cool
The mermaids keep
  A swimming school.

The oysters trot;
  The lobsters prance;
The dolphins come
  To join the dance.

But the jellyfish
  Who are rather small
Can't seem to learn
  The steps at all.

Marchette Chute

A Doll's Adventure at Sea
by Stephanie St. Pierre

ne fine summer day a crusty old crab crept along the sand at the edge of the sea. Soon he came to a very deep hole. At the bottom of the hole sat a sad little raggedy doll. Her clothes were wet and torn and her hair was tangled with seaweed. The little doll was frightened. She tried to be brave but she could not hold back her tears.

"I want to go home," cried the doll.

"Hello," said the crab, peering down at her from the edge of the hole. "Can I help you out?"

"Oh, please!" said the doll. The crab reached his long, prickly claw into the hole and the doll held on tight. Soon she was standing beside him on the sand. "Thank you so much," she said, wiping away her tears. "My name is Ellie."

"And where is your home, Ellie?" asked the crab. "You don't look like a crab or a fish. I don't think you belong in the sea, and I've never seen a creature like you in the sand."

"I am a *doll*," said Ellie. "And I belong with the little girl who loves me—the ferry captain's daughter. Every morning we ride the ferry together, but this morning I peeked over the railing to look at the sea and then . . . I fell in." Ellie almost began to cry again just thinking about it.

The crab was a softhearted fellow and he felt sorry for the little doll. "We will have to talk to Sally. She is the wisest creature in the sea." The crab scuttled across the sand toward the waves. He disappeared into the water for a moment but soon returned. With him came an enormous green turtle. Ellie told the wise old turtle her sad tale.

"We will need more help," said Sally. In no time the beach was full of creatures. "It is too far to swim," said Sally. "And Ellie is too heavy for the gulls to carry." Sally thought hard for a long time. "In the morning, Ellie will return to her boat," she said finally. "I have a plan, but all of you must help." Sally sent the creatures scurrying in all different directions. "In the meantime," said Sally to Ellie, "we will get you ready." The lobsters used their claws to pick the seaweed from Ellie's hair and comb it out into long golden curls. The sea gulls brought tiny shells and feathers to decorate Ellie's torn dress. Soon she looked like a brand-new doll. But would the other creatures get their work done in time for Ellie to reach the ferry? Ellie fell asleep waiting.

A gull's cry woke Ellie. A noisy crowd huddled around Sally. There was a lot of commotion as one more gull flew into the midst of the circle. Then suddenly it was quiet. Ellie noticed that the sun was beginning to rise—the boat would be coming soon! Ellie shook her head sadly. How could they make it in time? She slowly walked toward Sally, ready to accept the news that she would not be going home after all. But then...

Ellie could not believe her eyes. In front of her a bright red balloon rose up in the air. Beneath it bobbed a small basket, just large enough for a little doll! A dozen crabs held the basket down by long strings clamped in their strong claws.

"Hurry," said Sally. "Hop in and let the wind give you a ride. The gulls will steer you." Ellie ran to the basket and climbed in. One by one the crabs let go of their strings. The big red balloon began to rise, higher and higher, until it was sailing high over the sea.

"Thank you all," shouted Ellie to her friends below on the beach. "Good-bye." Before long the boat came into view. With the sea gulls' help Ellie was soon hovering over the deck. Ellie saw a little girl looking sadly out to sea—her very own little girl.

"It's her," Ellie cried. "But it's too far to jump. How will I..." Suddenly she heard a loud POP! Then she was falling, falling, falling...straight into the arms of the startled little girl. "Oh, Ellie! My Ellie is back!" cried the little girl with joy. "Never ever leave me again."

And the little doll never did.

SIMPLY SILLY SEASIDE RIDDLES

Jennifer: **This is a friendly beach!**
Daniel: How can you tell?
Jennifer: *I just saw the ocean wave!*

What kind of star
comes out in the daytime?
A starfish.

What has 8 arms and
carries 50 people?
An octobus.

How can you tell if there's been a shark in your refrigerator? *There are a thousand teethmarks in the meatloaf.*

What did one fish say to the other fish? *Let's go people-ing!*

What would you do if a whale sat in front of you in the movies? *Miss most of the movie.*

Merla
the Mischievous Mermaid
by Laura Hitchcock

 n an ocean cove not far away and not so long ago, there lived a little mermaid. Her name was Merla, and like all mermaids, she was a girl from the waist up. Below the waist, she had the shimmery body of a fish.

Although Merla looked like other mermaids, she didn't act like one. Most mermaids were calm and gentle and wise. But Merla was nothing but mischievous! Day and night, she loved to play tricks on all the other creatures in the sea.

Every day Merla raced through underwater caves at top speed, calling, "Look out! Here I come!" All the fish darted out of her way. And if she thought up a good joke, she just had to tell someone. So she woke up the oysters, who had just gone to bed.

"When does a fish go to the doctor?" she asked the oysters.

"We don't know and we don't care," the oysters answered sleepily.

But Merla didn't listen. "When he's feeling eel!" she said, laughing. Then she plucked a pearl from an oyster's shell and took it away to play catch with.

Merla liked to tease humans, too. Whenever she saw a small boat sailing by, she came up for air and smacked her tail on the water. The humans screamed and stood up to see what had made such a noise—so Merla rocked the boat to make them dizzy! Oh, was she a pest!

Of course, news of this mischief got back to the Fish Council. Soon the Fish Council was holding emergency meetings every week, just to hear the complaints! Merla was ordered to appear before them.

"Don't you remember your duty as a mermaid?" asked the oldest, wisest fish. "You're supposed to help your fellow fish—and fellow humans, too—not play tricks!"

"I know," said Merla. "But I get so excited, and then—"

"Think!" the oldest, wisest fish interrupted. "Think before you pull your tricks! And then think again!"

Merla tried to remember his advice: "Think and think again!" Whenever she had an urge to play a trick, she stopped and thought about it. Then she thought about it again. But all she could think of were even better tricks to play!

Once she saw the octopus and thought it would be funny to tickle him under all eight of his arms. But she stopped herself. "Think and think again!" she reminded herself. So she thought and thought, and decided it would be even funnier if she tied his arms in knots!

"Merla, you are one naughty mermaid!" called the octopus angrily as Merla swam away.

The Fish Council called Merla to appear one last time.

"We've given you every chance, Merla," sighed the oldest, wisest fish. "But you just don't behave. Maybe you can find other fish, somewhere else, who will appreciate your jokes."

Poor Merla. She swam to the surface, slowly, to take one last look at her beloved ocean cove.

When she popped her head out of the water, she was surprised to see the sky and ocean growing dark. The wind blew, whistling, over huge, rolling waves. Merla knew a storm was on the way.

Suddenly, Merla spotted something strange. It was a tiny boat, far out to sea, tossing up and down. Inside were a man and a small boy, waving for help.

Quick as a flash, Merla swam to the boat. She tugged, trying to pull it to shore. But the boat was too heavy for one lone mermaid. "Think and think again," thought Merla. She thought and thought hard. All at once she knew exactly what to do. She turned, dived, and raced back to the Fish Council.

"Emergency at sea!" Merla shouted to the Fish Council. "A boat's in trouble in a storm!"

Everyone rushed to the surface with Merla. "What should we do?" asked a seahorse.

Merla thought and thought again, and came up with a plan. "Octopus!" she shouted. "Hold the boat with your arms and pull. Everyone else swim under the boat to guide it to shore!"

When the little boy saw the octopus grab his boat, he screamed with fright. "Think and think again," thought Merla, and soon she knew how to calm the boy down. She swam next to the boat and

told silly jokes. Soon the boy was giggling as the fish pushed the boat out of the storm.

When they reached the shore, the boy and man thanked all the sea creatures for saving them.

"Thank Merla," said the oldest, wisest fish. "She had all the good ideas."

"I have to thank all of you," Merla said to the sea creatures, "for putting up with all my tricks. Now I know that thinking can be put to good use and not just mischief!"

The oldest, wisest fish presented Merla with a special shell, a medal of the highest honor.

"This is for thinking and thinking again!" he said. And all the sea creatures clapped.

Little People™ Big Book About THE SEA

TIME-LIFE for CHILDREN™

Publisher: Robert H. Smith
Managing Editor: Neil Kagan
Associate Editors: Jean Burke Crawford,
Patricia Daniels
Marketing Director: Ruth P. Stevens
Promotion Director: Kathleen B. Tresnak
Associate Promotion Director: Jane B. Welihozkiy
Production Manager: Prudence G. Harris
Editorial Consultants: Jacqueline A. Ball,
Sara Mark

PRODUCED BY PARACHUTE PRESS, INC.

Editorial Director: Joan Waricha
Editors: Christopher Medina, Jane Stine, Wendy Wax
Writers: Cathy Dubowski, Shirley Albert,
Laura Hitchcock, Michael J. Pellowski,
Stephanie St. Pierre, Natalie Standiford,
Jean Waricha
Designer: Michel Design
Illustrators: Meg Aubrey, Yvette Banek,
Pat and Robin DeWitt, Jeff DiNardo,
Heather King, Turi Macombie,
John Speirs, John Wallner, Linda Weller

Time-Life Books Inc. is a wholly owned subsidary of
THE TIME INC. BOOK COMPANY.

TIME-LIFE is a trademark of Time Warner Inc.
U.S.A.

FISHER-PRICE, LITTLE PEOPLE and AWNING
DESIGN are trademarks of Fisher-Price, Division of
The Quaker Oats Company and are used under
license.

Time-Life Books Inc. offers a wide range of fine
publications, including home video products. For
subscription information, call 1-800-621-7026, or
write TIME-LIFE BOOKS, P.O. Box C-32068, Rich-
mond, Virginia 23261-2068.

ACKNOWLEDGMENTS

Every effort has been made to trace the ownership of all copyrighted material and to secure the necessary
permissions to reprint these selections. If any question arises as to the use of any material, the editor and the
publisher, while expressing regret for any inadvertent error, will make the necessary correction in future
printings.

Grateful acknowledgment is made to the following for permission to reprint copyrighted material: Harper &
Row for "The Fish With the Deep Sea Smile" from NIBBLE, NIBBLE by Margaret Wise Brown. Copyright ©
1959 by William R. Scott, Inc. Homeland Publishing, a division of Troubadour Records Ltd. for "Baby Beluga,"
words by Raffi, D. Pike. Copyright © 1980 Homeland Publishing. Houghton Mifflin Co. for "The Vision in
the Snow" from SEABIRD, text and illustrations by Holling C. Holling. Copyright © 1948, 1974 by Holling C.
Holling; and "Sea Shell" from THE COMPLETE POETIC WORKS OF AMY LOWELL by Amy Lowell. Copyright © 1955 by Houghton Mifflin Co., renewed 1983 by Houghton Mifflin Co., Brinton P. Roberts, Esq. and
G. D'Andelot Belin, Esq. Gina Maccoby Literary Agency for "Fish" from HELLO AND GOOD-BY by Mary
Ann Hoberman. Copyright © 1959, 1987 by Mary Ann Hoberman. Mary Britton Miller Estate for "Shore"
by Mary Britton Miller. Copyright © Estate of Mary Britton Miller. Mary Chute Smith for "Undersea" by
Marchette Chute, from PIPER PIPE THAT SONG AGAIN, published by Random House. Copyright © Mary
Chute Smith.

Library of Congress Cataloging-in-Publication Data

Little people big book about the sea.

(Little people big books)
Summary: An illustrated collection of stories, essays, songs, poems, activities, and games featuring the sea and its
inhabitants.
1. Ocean—Literary collections. [1. Ocean—Literary collections] I. Time-Life for Children (Firm)
II. Title: About the sea. III. Series.
PZ5.L72587 1989   810.8′036   89-20542
ISBN 0-8094-7475-1
ISBN 0-8094-7476-X (lib. bdg.)

TIME-LIFE BOOKS
ALEXANDRIA, VIRGINIA